CHILDREN OF THE WORLD BOOKS

HASSAN BOY OF THE DESERT

STORY
AND PHOTOGRAPHS
BY
DOMINIQUE
DARBOIS

Adapted from the French

FOLLETT PUBLISHING COMPANY
CHICAGO

& FERNAND NATHAN • PARIS

Library of Congress Catalog Card Number: 61-14401

Sixth Printing
ISBN 0 695-43680-5 Titan binding

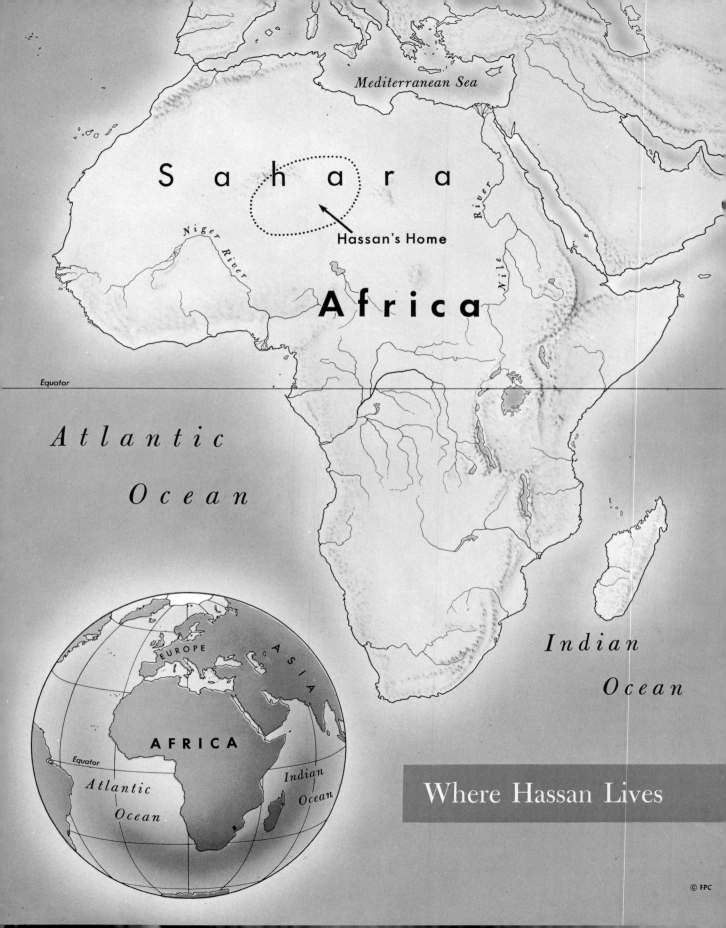

Mediterranean Sea

Sahara

Niger River

Hassan's Home

Africa

River

Nile

Equator

Atlantic

Ocean

Indian

Ocean

EUROPE

ASIA

AFRICA

Equator

Atlantic

Ocean

Indian

Ocean

Where Hassan Lives

© FPC

Hassan and his family live in a very hot and dry land in northern Africa. Day after day the only scenery they see is a large, sunburned desert. Because this desert is so empty the Arabs call it *sahrá,* meaning the "wilderness." We call it Sahara.

3

Hassan's family belongs to a tribe of desert people called the Tuaregs. Tuaregs are nomads, which means they wander over the desert in search of food and water.

Hassan's family knows from experience where to find places in the Sahara that have water and a few bushes and trees growing. A place like this is called an oasis and is very important. No person or animal can live long without water in the desert.

Today Hassan and his brother, Bedari, have awakened very early. They are going to harness a camel so that their father can ride to the market and trade.

They walk together to the camel herd. Here they find the animals still resting. Some of the camels are white like sugar. Others are yellow like sand or grey like iron.

These camels are important to Hassan's family. They carry heavy loads over the hot desert and provide meat to eat, hair for cloth, and milk that is very healthful to drink.

When Hassan stands beside his father's camel, he feels very small. But Hassan knows how to make the camel obey him.

"Sit," he orders while pulling on a rope tied to the camel's nose.

6

The camel has a hard time following Hassan's order. He can not easily lower himself since his legs are very long. But with clumsy movements he does manage to kneel on his forelegs. This does not hurt the camel, for his knees are covered with thick rolls of flesh. These rolls of flesh are very helpful when the camel has to kneel with heavy bundles on his back.

Then he sinks to the ground on his hind legs.

As soon as the camel is sitting on the sand, the boys begin to harness him. Hassan's two other brothers have brought a large leather bag. This bag contains the bridle and saddle.

Their father uses the bridle to tell the camel where to go. He can make the camel stop, start or go to the left or right by pulling the bridle different ways.

One of Hassan's brothers looks to be certain the bridle is securely fastened. Otherwise, it might become loose when his father guides the camel over the desert.

Finally the children are ready to tie the saddle on the camel's back. Hassan attaches a leather strap to one side of the saddle. Then he passes the strap under the camel's belly to his brother, who ties it to the other side of the saddle.

This saddle is carved from wood and looks like a small chair. It is beautifully decorated. Hassan's father carefully picked out the designs and colors by himself.

The camel is now completely harnessed, and Hassan is proud to have helped his brothers.

Their father arrives at the camel herd to inspect the boys' work.

10

Like all the men of the tribe, their father wears a veil over his face. Wearing veils has been the custom of the Tuaregs for hundreds of years. The Tuaregs are often called the "People of the Veil."

The veil is a piece of thin cotton cloth. It is several yards long and is twisted around the head and face. Usually only the eyes can be seen.

This veil and other garments of the Tuaregs are dyed blue with the wild indigo plant that grows in the oasis. The blue comes off on the Tuaregs when they wear the clothes. Little by little the dye colors the skin of the Tuaregs blue. For this reason they are called the "Blue Men."

When he has finished inspecting the harness,
Hassan's father climbs on the camel. Then Hassan
gets on behind his father.

When the boy is on, his father lets go of the camel's head. Quickly the animal rises to his feet and then starts across the desert. Hassan is careful to hold on to the back of the saddle tightly. Otherwise, he might fall off the fast-moving camel.

They are going to the market.

14

Hassan likes to go with his father to the market because it is always very interesting. Here people from all parts of the Sahara come to buy and sell animals, food, and other goods.

All the camels that are for sale are herded in one place. The horses and donkeys are grouped farther back. By keeping the animals separate a man has to look only at the kind of animal he wants to buy.

15

Hassan and his father examine the donkeys. Hassan's father wants to pick out a strong animal. Finally he buys a black one. A donkey is a good work animal and can live on little food.

The market is also the place to meet friends. Here the men tell about their recent travels and give news from other parts of the desert.

16

Since the market lasts for two days, Hassan's
father decides to stay near his camel herd for the
night. He rides his camel back to the herd while
Hassan follows him on the donkey.

Here they find the boy's mother watching the
camels. When Hassan's father tells her of his plan
to stay, she starts unpacking the tent.

17

The men start digging holes in the ground.
In the holes poles will be placed. The tent will
be tied to these poles. The poles are made from
the roots of a thorny bush that grows in the desert.
The tent is made from many goatskins.

18

This tent gives Hassan and his family shelter from the sun in the day and the cold at night. Although the desert is very hot during the day, the temperature drops rapidly after sunset. The desert is very cold at night.

19

During the day a dry wind blows over the Sahara. Usually it gives a pleasant relief from the heat.

Sometimes the wind blows very hard and carries large amounts of sand and dust with it. This wind is called the Sirocco, "wind from the south."

The Sirocco blows across the Sahara so strongly that it can tear a tent from its poles. Since a tent is the only shelter Hassan's parents have, they make sure theirs is tied very tightly to its poles. Otherwise, it might become undone and collapse in a strong wind.

20

After the tent is put up, Hassan's mother begins to unpack her cooking bowls, spoons, and straw mats. She will divide the tent into two sections. On one side she will put the straw mats that they sleep on. On the other side she will place her bowls, spoons, and other cooking needs.

While she is unpacking, she tells the children to get some water from a nearby well. First Hassan finds the donkey that is tied to one of the tent's poles. He places a bucket and water-skin on the animal.

Then Hassan, his brother Bedari, and the other children walk with the donkey to the well that is a mile from the tent.

When they reach the well, Hassan's sister
Karba drops the bucket made of goatskin into it.
This well is very deep, for the water is far below
the sand. Karba lowers the bucket almost 100 feet
before it touches the water.

While pulling it up, Karba is careful not to fall
into the well. For the bucket is heavy when filled
with water.

24

Karba pours the water into the waterskin that the other children hold.

This waterskin is made from a goatskin. Hassan's mother took the entire skin of a goat and placed it in the sun to dry. Then she sewed the goatskin's legs closed to make it watertight.

Karba has to lower and raise the bucket many times before the waterskin is filled. It can hold 25 quarts of water.

When the waterskin is finally full, the children tie its legs together. Then they bind the waterskin to the donkey with a rope.

Hassan and Karba climb on the animal and return to the tent with the water. The other children walk home.

Their mother has been cooking. She has placed a big, round pot on three stones. These stones keep the pot from resting in the fire.

She feeds the fire with camel dung that has been dried in the sun. This is the only fuel in the desert. Wood is very scarce.

She cooks barley with a little butter. When it is ready, Hassan and the other children sit in a circle and eat it from the same bowl with wooden spoons.

Then they drink camel's milk and eat dried dates.

After their meal the children sit together and play a game. They place little stones into holes they dug in the sand. Five stones are put into each hole. Then a player throws a stone in the air, hoping it will fall in one of the holes. If it does, he is allowed to take a stone out. The player with the most stones at the end of the game wins.

At the moment Hassan's brother is winning.

30

Soon the children get tired of this game. Next they place little pieces of straw against each other. They are trying to make the straws stand up by themselves.

Hassan plays for awhile, but then decides to go inside the tent. It is very hot at this time of day, and the tent shades him from the sun. A baby goat also comes into the shelter to keep cool.

32

His mother is inside the tent, making their beds. Two poles are put on the ground. Then sticks with round ends are placed across the poles. Over this wooden frame she rests the mats of braided straw.

Tonight her family will sleep away from the ground and the insects that live in the sand.

Then Hassan watches his mother prepare goat-skins for another tent. The skins already have been dried and the hair removed.

They have been smeared with butter to make them waterproof. Now she sews the edges of two skins together with tight stitches. She must sew 20 skins to make one tent.

It is time to give the camels water. So the children go to the camel herd and lead the animals to the well.

Hassan, Karba, and their brother ride two of the camels there. The other children guide the rest of the herd with ropes.

Camels are called the "ships of the desert" because they can travel great distances over the desert while carrying heavy loads on their backs. Since their feet have thick wide pads on them, the animals do not sink into the loose sand. Also camels can run quite fast, if they are not carrying too many waterskins and bags.

Before going on a long trip, a camel will do nothing but eat and drink for days. A camel can store enough water in his body to last him for several days.

A camel also stores food in his hump, where it stays in the form of fat. As the camel uses up this fat on a trip, the hump loses its firm shape and drops to one side in folds.

One of the camels strays from the herd to eat the leaves of a thorny shrub. Camels will eat anything that grows on the desert.

When Hassan returns to the tent, his mother gives him a bath in a small pan. Like the rest of the family Hassan takes only a few baths a year. He and his people consider water as precious as gold and like to use it only for drinking.

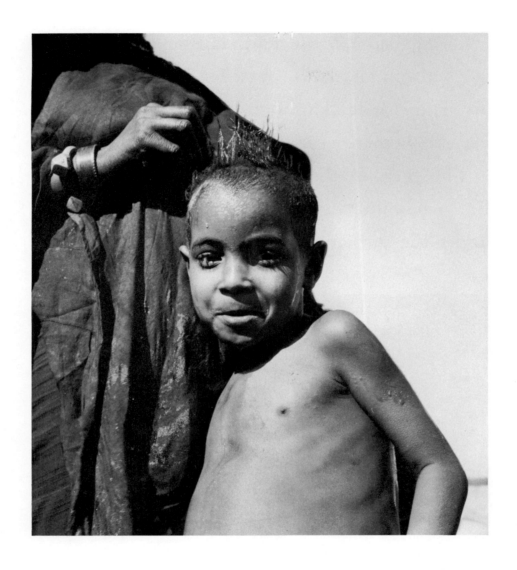

After the bath his mother rubs butter over his body. If this is not done, his skin becomes very dry. The burning sun is very hard on the skin, and butter helps to protect it.

41

Going back to the tent, Hassan sits with his mother and sister. He watches his mother braid his sister's hair. Although it takes a long time to fix, the women wear their hair in tiny braids.

The men of the tribe wear their hair loose. But when they grow up, their hair is hidden under the turban.

Now the sun is starting to set. All the men sit in front of the tent to discuss their day at the market and to have some tea. Hassan and his sister join the men and listen to the news.

One man breaks a loaf of sugar he bought at the market into small pieces. He places these white and shining pieces of sugar and some tea leaves into a small teapot.

He adds water and lets the tea brew for a few minutes. When the tea is ready, he serves it according to their custom.

He holds the teapot high in the air and pours a stream of golden brown tea into a glass. The smell is delicious.

After Hassan drinks his tea, he falls asleep.

Tomorrow he and his family will pack their possessions on the camels and wander over the Sahara. When they find an oasis, they will stop for a few days to graze their animals and fill their waterskins.

Then Hassan and his family will continue to wander over the Sahara.